Information Security
JumpStart Guide

Non-Profit Edition

ISBN 978-1-387-71864-1

Contents

About the Author 5

Foreward 7

Introduction 9

Why worry about an Information Security Program? 11

    Three Primary Reasons 11

        Regulatory 11

        Industry 13

        Organizational 13

    Glossary of Key Requirements and Standards 14

        HIPAA / HITECH 14

        PCI DSS 15

        FERPA 16

        NIST 800-53 16

        ISO 27001 16

        Cyber Risk Insurance Requirements 17

        Other 17

    How to Determine Which Requirements Apply to You 18

    Helpful Skills For Improving Your Security Posture 19

Five Steps to a Better Information Security Posture 20

    Step 1A: Communicate With Your Organization 21

    Step 1B: Assess Your Biggest Risks 22

        Inventory Data at Rest 23

        Inventory Data in Transit 23

        Inventory Computer Systems and Computing Devices 24

        Inventory Computer Applications 24

Inventory Paper Records...25

Inventory Prying Eyes..25

Inventory People...26

Inventory System Access Control......................................26

Inventory Other Technology infrastructure.....................27

Assess the Inventory 27

Step 2: Take Action – First Four Actions for Risk Reduction..27

Application Whitelisting..28

Application Patching 28

OS Patching 29

Minimize Admin Privileges...29

Step 3A: Take Action – Establish Processes, Policies and
Procedures 31

Policies 31

Processes and Procedures 32

Step 3B: Conduct Training For Everyone in the Organization 34

Step 4A: Take Action – Test Your Environment 35

Backups - Try a Test Restore 35

Vulnerability Testing – External and Internal....................37

Penetration Testing (by a Third Party) 38

Social Engineering Testing 38

Step 4B: Train Your Organization Again...............................40

Step 5: Set Up for Ongoing Maintenance 40

Establish a Calendar 41

Execute and Keep Score..42

Review at End of Year and Revise 43

Final Thoughts...44

For more information 45

   ISACA...45

   ISC^2 45

   InfraGard 45

   SANS 46

   NIST 46

   ISSA 46

   HIMSS..46

   CHIME 47

   NIST HIPAA Toolkit 47

   NIST CyberSecurity Control Framework (MS Excel Format) .. 47

   NIST Special Publications 47

References 47

About the Author

Blake Holman is currently Chief Information Officer and HIPAA Security Officer at St. David's Foundation in Austin, Texas, a position he has held since September, 2015. Prior to St. David's Foundation, Blake served as Sr. Vice President and Chief Information Officer at Ryan, LLC in Dallas, Texas.

Blake has over 25 years of experience leading Information Technology Strategy, Development and Operations for several organizations in Consulting, Telecommunications, Financial Services and Non-profit Healthcare.

Blake holds a Bachelor of Science degree in Mechanical Engineering from Southern Methodist University, and a Strategic IT Management Certificate from the Scandinavian International Management Institute in Copenhagen, Denmark. Blake is currently working on a Master of Science degree in Information Security and Assurance at Western Governor's University. Blake holds a number of industry certifications including the CEH, CHFI, C-CISO, CISM and CISSP certifications related to Information Security.

In 2011 and 2012, Blake's efforts were recognized in the InformationWeek 500 listing of the most innovative business technology companies in the United States. In 2011, Blake's employer, Ryan was ranked 130th, and in 2012, Ryan's ranking rose to 98th. In both cases, Ryan was the highest ranked corporate tax services firm on the list.

In December 2012, Blake was named by Computerworld magazine as one of its 2013 "Premier 100 IT Leaders." The Computerworld Premier 100 IT recognition is an international lifetime award that shines a spotlight on technology and business leaders from a broad range of organizations.

In October 2017, Blake co-authored the second edition of a book entitled "What Every Engineer Should Know About Excel". This work was originally published by his late father, Dr. Jack Holman, who was a world renowned professor of Mechanical Engineering at SMU.

In November 2017, Blake was recognized by the Austin Chapter of the Society for Information Management as the Public Sector IT Executive of the Year in Austin, Texas at the 20th Annual Austin Innotech Conference.

Outside the world of technology, Blake and his wife Joan enjoy travelling and completing half marathons. Blake is a retired Rugby player, enjoys supporting his Rugby Club and the sport of Rugby at every available opportunity, including cheering on his son John, who actively plays rugby in Texas.

Foreward

Why care about information security if you are a non-profit? The answer is simple. Information is power. In a world where non-profits are being called upon to do more for more people it will become increasingly more important to protect the data obtained and produced because of your work. However, for many in the non-profit sector the topic of information security may sound like something the government or corporations have the capability to do something about. In this guide Blake Holman begins to peel back the layers on how your organization can begin asking the right questions of itself as it prepares to strengthen its information security infrastructure.

Blake and I have worked together for almost two years. In that time a couple of things have become clear. First, Blake is an expert in the field of information technology. He has over two decades in the field with some very prominent technology companies. He has also helped the St. David's Foundation build out its technology infrastructure to meet the challenges of fast growing and complex philanthropic organization. Second, he has the heart for the field of philanthropy. One definition of philanthropy is the act or gift done or made for humanitarian purposes. Blake has shown this in his work. He has taken his expertise, without direction or expectation, and provided much needed wisdom and guidance to non-profits with technology questions or problems to solve.

In this guide Blake takes complex issues and puts them in an easy to follow format. If you are like many of us, you may struggle with forming the beginning questions as it relates to information security. He even helps the reader structure the right questions to ask depending on the need. Granted, you will not be an expert by the end of reading this guide. However, you will at least know where to begin. So, grab your senior and IT staff, make sure the coffee is fresh, take a deep breath and take your first steps in leading your organization into the technological 21st century.

Enjoy!

William M. Buster
Executive Vice President for Community Investments
St. David's Foundation
Austin, Texas

Introduction

Non-profit organizations everywhere have the same Information Security challenges that for-profit organizations have, though they often have fewer human and financial resources with which to address these challenges.

This guide is written for those organizations that know they need to do something about Information Security, but aren't sure where to start. This guide provides a place to start and get moving in the right direction toward protecting the organization's information. Rome wasn't built in a day, nor should an organization expect to snap their fingers and suddenly have a comprehensive security program in place.

Though this guide is not a comprehensive Information Security reference, nor does it provide a roadmap to certification against any of the standards discussed herein, it is also not intended to position an organization to pass a security audit. However, when an organization knows they need to do something and doesn't know where to start, this guide gets them started toward making a material improvement in their Information Security posture.

In the sections that follow, I outline several recommended steps to an improved security posture, I outline a simple way to setup maintenance of an Information Security program, and I offer references to a vast array of information and resources for the reader to consider.

I have had the pleasure of working with several non-profit organizations in helping them improve their security posture, and it is my sincere desire that this guide can help many, many more.

Finally, a web site has been established to accompany this guide. That site can be reached at: http://securityguide.blakeholman.com.

Blake K. Holman
2/17/2018
Austin, Texas

Why worry about an Information Security Program?

There are many reasons that a non-profit organization may need to worry about having an Information Security Program. The sections that follow indicate some of these reasons, including what can happen if an organization doesn't worry about having a program. In addition, we provide a short glossary of some of the key regulations / standards in existence today, and then provide some guidance on how to determine which, if any, apply to your organization.

While compliance with regulatory or industry pressures may be a requirement, achieving compliance won't happen over-night. If an organization has nothing in place today, this Guide serves as a way to get started that will add value and focus regardless of what is driving the organization to comply.

Three Primary Reasons

There are three primary reasons to worry about having an Information Security program. The first is for regulatory reasons. The second is for reasons involving industry pressure. The third reason is simply for compliance with your organization's contract and / or grant agreements. Bear in mind that these reasons are not necessarily mutually exclusive. In other words, your organization may have all three reasons as drivers to have an Information Security program in place. If that's the case, one investment in setting up your Information Security Program can extend benefit across all these risk categories.

Regulatory

A number of regulatory pressures exist, all of which put varying pressures on organizations to implement and maintain good Information Security programs. Two of the most well-known are the Health Insurance Portability and Accountability Act (HIPAA) and the Family Educational Rights and Privacy Act (FERPA). HIPAA applies to electronic protected health information and FERPA applies to educational records.

Related to HIPAA, in the event of a reported or suspected breach of an organization's EPHI, the US Health and Human Services (US HHS) organization has the ability to conduct a HIPAA audit on the organization in question. If this is your organization, the expectation by HHS is that you will have conducted a risk assessment, you'll have an Information Security Program in place and that you're maintaining that program on an ongoing basis.

HIPAA violations can carry with them some pretty steep penalties. In June 2017, MedPro published twenty brief accounts of penalties levied for HIPAA violations including, but not limited to, the following:

1. A UCLA surgeon was fined and jailed for illegally accessing Health records of his supervisor, co-workers and several celebrities.
2. A dermatology practice lost an unencrypted USB drive with patient records on it and was levied a fine of $150,000.
3. The State of New Jersey pursue a medical license suspension of a Doctor that forwarded patient bills for collections to an outside agency without "cleansing" them of electronic protected health information.
4. A Walgreens Pharmacist, in 2014, shared confidential medical information about a customer that once dated her husband. In this case, Walgreen was held liable and it led to a $1.4 million settlement award.
5. An employee of a cardiac monitoring vendor had a laptop with hundreds of patient medical records on it. This laptop was stolen from a parked car. The Federal Government reached a $2.5 million settlement with the

vendor, demonstrating that they're serious about protecting patients' health information.

Industry

There are some industries whose pressure to have good Information Security programs is driven more by industry pressure than regulation, though that line is blurring as governments begin to enact penalties for organizational failure to comply. The biggest industry in which this applies is the Financial Services industry, and the most well-known requirement is the Payment Card Industry Data Security Standard (PCI DSS).

PCI DSS violations are associated with breaches in credit card information and can carry with them steep penalties. The Focus on PCI organization indicates that fines for PCI DSS violations include, but are not limited to, the following:

1. Fines for non-compliance itself, range from $5,000 per month to $100,000 per month, depending on how many months the organization is non-compliant as well as the volume of credit card numbers that are in their possession.
2. Fines for a breach, even if the organization is 100% PCI compliant! Such fines can be up to $90 per card number breached. Then there is the cost of notifying each card holder, and implementing credit card monitoring services for each cardholder – the costs rack up quickly.

Organizational

Many organizations today do business with other organizations that have concerns over information security. In addition, more and more organizations are carrying Cyber Risk insurance as a way to protect the organization in the case of a data breach. Contract or Grant Agreements between organizations are increasingly including requirements to have Information

Security programs in place, as are Cyber Risk Insurance programs. If your organization has a contract with another that has Cyber Risk requirements on them, they will often extend to your organization, sometimes without you knowing it.

With organizational drivers, the consequences of not having a good Information Security program in place are more black-and-white. For example, if a Grant agreement requires your organization to have a program and it doesn't, it is in violation of the agreement and the funding is at risk of being pulled. Since many non-profit organizations live and die by their grant funding, such consequences can be quite severe.

Glossary of Key Requirements and Standards
The sections that follow outline some of the key standards, regulations or sources of pressure from outside an organization for it to take action.

HIPAA / HITECH
HIPAA is the Health Insurance Portability and Accountability Act. The US Health and Human Services web site, http://HHS.gov, provides the reader a good introduction to and background on HIPAA / HITECH for information beyond this guide. HIPAA was enacted in 1996 and consists of five sections, or Titles. Title II has to do with Administrative Simplification, though there isn't anything really simple about its provisions. Title II has numerous subsections in it, though the two most applicable sections for the world of Information Security are the Privacy Rule and the Security Rule. The Privacy rule calls for protection of all Protected Health Information (PHI), whether on paper or in electronic form. The Security Rule complements the Privacy Rule in that it governs Electronic Protected Health Information (EPHI) and calls for Administrative Safeguards, Physical Safeguards and Technical Safeguards regarding how the

complying organization will meet or exceed the requirements of HIPAA.

HITECH is the Health Information Technology for Economic and Clinical Health Act. HITECH was enacted to promote improved use of Information Technology in Healthcare and sets meaningful use and interoperability provisions for Electronic Health Records (EHR) systems. Included in Subtitle D of HITECH are improved provisions related to HIPAA Privacy and Security.

In the case of a data breach, a number of parties are affected. The organization itself is affected, patients whose information was breached are affected and leadership and Board members of the organization are affected. The penalties for failure to comply with HIPAA and HITECH regulations can be quite steep, as can the costs of notifying everyone whose information was breached. In addition, the cost of dealing with a public relations challenge like this can be quite large. For smaller organizations, the penalties and costs can result in the organization having to close its doors.

PCI DSS

PCI DSS is the Payment Card Industry Data Security Standard, now in release version 3.2 (as of April 2016). PCI DSS is an information security standard related to credit cards. It is required by the card brands (predominantly MasterCard, Visa, American Express and Discover) and overseen by the Payment Card Industry Security Standards Council.

Like HIPAA and HITECH, the penalties for failure to comply can be quite high, particularly if a breach is involved. The state of California, at one time for example, levied its own penalties of up to $20,000 per incident in the case of breached credit card information. In this scenario, a single credit card number was considered an incident. If 100,000 card numbers were breached, the penalty would be $2 billion.

While compliance isn't a guarantee of not being breached, it is a suitable risk mitigation strategy and is a major consideration associated with penalties when a breach is experienced. If your organization handles credit cards for the sale of goods or accepting donations, you need to be aware of the PCI DSS requirements.

FERPA

FERPA is the Family Educational Rights and Privacy Act. FERPA, Enacted in 1974, is a US federal law that governs the access to educational information and records for public entities. Examples of such are potential employers, publically funded educational institutions, and foreign governments. Of particular interest related to Information Security is the protection of Personally Identifiable Information (PII) in this act, as well as the protection of student medical records that may be maintained by educational institutions as part of a student's records.

NIST 800-53

NIST 800-53 refers to NIST Special Publication 800-53. It is a catalog of security controls for use with United States Federal Government information systems except for those that relate to National Security. It is one of many special publications published by the National Institute of Standards, and though it is aimed at governmental use, it is a phenomenal reference of information security controls. Many organizations have turned to NIST 800-53 as a guide for their information security control programs because it has great depth and breadth.

Vast amounts of information are available at the Computer Security Resource Center at https://csrc.nist.gov/publications/sp800.

ISO 27001

ISO27001 refers to ISO/IEC 27001, which is an information security standard that specifies a management system intended to bring information security under management control. This standard, like NIST 800-53, gives specific requirements, and an organization implementing it can seek certification and accreditation by an external certifying body. There is often significant expense in using ISO 27001 and seeking certification under such, which has driven a number of organizations to utilize NIST 800-53, which is equally useful as an information security control reference.

Cyber Risk Insurance Requirements

Any organization that carries Cyber Risk Insurance will have requirements for having at least a basic Information Security program in order to maintain the insurance and minimize risk. While those requirements vary by Insurance Carrier, alignment to an industry standard or a regulatory requirement is like an "easy button" for compliance. Fundamentally, the principles of good Information Security programs are consistent, though different references may put their particular "flavor" on them. As an example, the fundamental security requirements of PCI DSS and HIPAA overlap significantly, though one clearly is concerned with credit card data and the other is concerned with electronic protected health information. Should an organization comply with one or the other, they will undoubtedly have an excellent posture related to any requirements that Cyber Risk Insurance might put on the organization.

Other

Of course, the references here are not an exhaustive list of industry and regulatory pressures that are driving organizations to formalize their information security programs and have maintenance programs in place. The landscape is constantly evolving as are the technologies available for both attacking and protecting our organizations' information.

At the end of this document, there are a number of references to organizations and resources for further information related to Information Security. They also serve as great sources of information about the ongoing landscape changes that organizations should keep in mind now and in the future.

How to Determine Which Requirements Apply to You

Ask yourself some simple questions to determine which reasons apply to your organization for having an Information Security Program in place. These questions include:

1. Does my organization create, possess, receive and/or store protected health information of any person or persons for any reason whatsoever? If so, you must be HIPAA compliant.
2. Does my organization possess or process credit card numbers for any reason whatsoever? If so, you must be PCI DSS compliant, and must go through a certification process.
3. Does my organization possess educational records? If so, FERPA is going to apply to you.
4. Does my organization carry Cyber Risk Insurance? If so, does that insurance require us to have an Information Security Program in place? If yes, you have to comply.
5. Does my organization receive Grant money from other organizations? If so, do the Grant agreements require us to have an Information Security Program in place? If yes, you have to comply.

As an additional note to item 1 above – let's say that your organization provides gap benefits to cover the expenses of a person related to your organization in association with health insurance deductibles, but they have to submit for expense reimbursements associated with those expenses. If the documentation of those expense reimbursements includes health information, like CPT codes, diagnoses, prescription information and such, then your organization is holding PHI and must consider being HIPAA compliant.

Helpful Skills For Improving Your Security Posture

While almost anyone can reasonably accomplish an improved security posture for an organization, with enough time and resources, the reality is that those with technical skills and experience in the realm of Information Security will have an easier time doing so. If your organization's intention is to attack this problem internally, it will be helpful for your IT support person or people (whether employees or hired from outside) to have some or many of the skills noted below. Bear in mind that all of these skills can be developed and are reinforced very well with the experience of implementing and maintaining an organization's security program as well as interacting with other similarly skilled professionals. As such, don't be overly concerned if your organization doesn't have access to these skills at the start of the effort.

Skills that will be helpful to improving an organization's Information Security posture include, but are not limited to, the following:

- Knowledge of and ability to identify components of IT infrastructure: servers, networks, firewalls, end user devices (laptops, desktops, mobile telephones), printers, multi-function devices (copier / scanners)
- Knowledge of and ability to identify End user applications
- Knowledge of and ability to identify Enterprise applications
- Detail oriented – need to be able to thoughtfully identify and document all the risk points of technology infrastructure and applications
- Ability to understand and respect risk
- Experience obtaining and applying OS and application patches, preferably in an automated manner, though manual is sufficient for small environments
- Experience administering systems from a user and access control perspective

- Experience backing up and restoring data and systems
- Experience with IT policies and procedures highly desired
- Experience with IT processes highly desired (perhaps even specify ITIL – the IT Infrastructure Library)
- Experience with different IT Security Control Frameworks highly desired – NIST 800-53, ISO27000 Series and/or others
- Experience having been through an Information Security Audit highly desired
- Action oriented rather than someone who suffers from "analysis paralysis"

Five Steps to a Better Information Security Posture

Information Security is important for every organization that uses technology and information. The proliferation of computers and computing devices has dramatically increased the risk of information ending up some place that it shouldn't. And the world is becoming less tolerant of breaches in Information Security.

The sections that follow outline five key steps (see Figure 1) that an organization can take to materially impact their Information Security posture in a positive way (i.e. reduced risk). Organizations are strongly encouraged to take all five steps, understanding that taking shortcuts will simply limit the risk reduction for that organization.

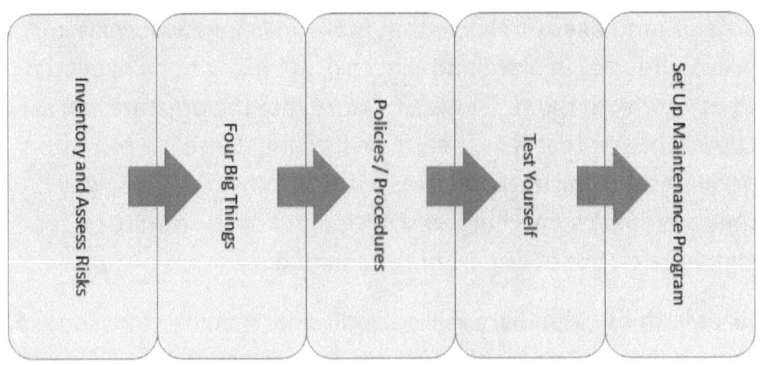

Figure 1: JumpStart Steps to Improved Information Security

Step 1A: Communicate With Your Organization

As we take this journey toward improving the Information Security posture of your organization, we will call out several times that there is only so much that we can do with computers and such to reduce risk. The reality is that people are also a big part of our risk profile. As such, establishing initial communication to your organization, preferably in the form of an interactive training, will serve the organization well.

The objective of the initial communication training is to inform them on what the organization intends to do, or maybe must do, how they will go about doing it and what every person is expected to do to help support the effort. For example, let's say that a non-profit organization provides services to unwed mothers and has electronic protected health information as part of delivering those services.

This non-profit, by the nature of what they do, must comply with HIPAA. Non-profit leadership may know this and know what HIPAA is, but the rest of the organization may not fully understand it. By training the organization on what HIPAA is and what it means, why the organization must comply and what the organization is going to do to comply, everyone in the organization is better informed. Then, everyone in the organization needs to know that there will be new policies and procedures put in place and that they are going to be expected to comply with them. This is to ensure that the organization is compliant and that it can maintain its compliance. All too often organizations roll out initiatives without fully explaining why they are doing something, and miss a great opportunity to get everyone on board as part of the solution.

Later in this guide, there will be additional training steps to take, though they will be much more focused on action that everyone in the organization must take rather than this initial communication and awareness.

Step 1B: Assess Your Biggest Risks

One of the most important steps in getting started toward establishing an information security program (or improving one) is to conduct a risk assessment. Unfortunately, many organizations today respond to the hype of the industry and just start shopping for tools and spending money without validating where their risks are. This often results in spending a lot of time and money on things that may or may not materially improve the organization's risk posture, though they certainly help boost the revenue of companies that sell security tools and services.

The reader will be well-served to take the time, even if it is just a few thoughtful hours, to conduct an inventory of the potential risk points for their organization. Though every organization is different, there are many similarities in that they have the same types of things to worry about. The sections below outline many areas that should be considered in a risk inventory, and serve as a great place to start, if no other guidance is available.

For the inventory steps below, a sample inventory checklist is available at http://securityguide.blakeholman.com along with numerous other references and templates to aid in the process of improving your Information Security program.

Inventory Data at Rest

Data at rest is data stored on various forms of media. Media could be a spinning disk in a computer, a solid-state disk in a computer, a compact-disc or a DVD disc, a USB drive, an iPhone, a floppy disk (think 1980's) or even magnetic tape. This is not a complete list, rather provides the plethora of places on which data can be stored. It is referred to as being "at rest" when it is not actively being used by a computer program.

The most common items of concern for the risk inventory in this category are disks internal to servers and user workstations, removable disks (floppy disks, USB drives, compact discs, DVD discs) and tape media. The first step should be to inventory what you have and where it is. While inventorying, make note of whether the data is encrypted on those items – you'll need it for your risk assessment later.

In recent years, technology has evolved, particularly related to Cloud and SaaS architectures, to include in-memory databases and in-memory filesystems. While of potential concern from a security perspective, in-memory constructs are typically considered in the realm of data-in-use rather than data-at-rest. Still, situations where an organization utilizes in-memory databases or in-memory filesystems at Cloud or SaaS providers should be noted on the risk inventory as such.

Inventory Data in Transit

Data in transit is data that is travelling from one location to another. The most common reference to data in transit is data being transmitted over a network of some form, whether it be a local area network (LAN), metropolitan area network (MAN), wide area network (WAN) or even a personal area network (PAN). The media forms can be wired, wireless and can employ any number of potential protocols. Fundamentally, though, data in transit is data that is moving from one place to another.

The most common items of concern for the risk inventory in this category are the various area networks mentioned above. Inventory all network links, including Bluetooth connections and ad-hoc wireless network connections (sometimes used between workstations and printers). These are all potential places that sensitive data can be breached, depending on what your organization does to protect these links.

Inventory Computer Systems and Computing Devices

Computer systems refer to servers and workstations primarily. However, with the explosion of personal devices, organizations are increasingly needing to worry about devices. "Devices" include mobile telephones, tablets, E-book readers and even smart watches (think the Apple Watch). These devices are all capable of interfacing with each other and computer systems and can become a source of a breach of sensitive information.

Take inventory of every computer and device in use in your environment. Make sure you make note of any printer devices, including multi-function printer / scanner devices, as they have hard disks in them that can have copies of documents that were either printed or scanned on that device. If that hard disk leaves the premises, data can be retrieved and potentially breached.

Inventory Computer Applications

Computer applications run on computer systems and computing devices. These are things like Microsoft Word, Excel, Adobe Acrobat, and a number of other possible tools that are aimed at improving the efficiency and effectiveness of a computer user. In today's world of the consumerization of IT, individuals are more computer savvy and can easily search the Internet for tools to help make their lives easier. Unfortunately, hackers know this and can easily package up malicious code inside of a very useful tool and create a real problem from a security perspective.

For risk inventory purposes, take a good inventory of every application in use on every computer system or computing device in your enterprise. There will be many of them that you know about and endorse. However, you will also be surprised at how many applications (apps) users have downloaded trying to solve a problem and which pose a potential risk to your organization. Having this list of applications enables you to plug those holes and reduce that risk.

Again, for application inventory purposes, your inventory actions should extend to all potential computing devices as well. As noted in the Computer Systems and Computing Devices section above – every device is a potential risk, therefore, no device is exempt from being assessed.

Inventory Paper Records

While not a big deal for those information security standards that focus on electronic records, things like HIPAA Privacy do have a component of concern over paper records.

For your inventory, think about the paper records you have – both official and unofficial. Official records will be those that you have, that you file and that you presumably have a retention policy for – in other words, you keep them around for reference purposes or because someone (like the IRS) requires it.

Unofficial records are copies of official records that someone may have printed or copied and may have sitting in a pile on their desk, or they're carrying back and forth in a briefcase, or might be in an inter-office envelope moving from one department to another.

Inventory Prying Eyes

Prying eyes refers to those situations where someone who is working with sensitive data has it up on their computer screen, and someone else is "looking over their shoulder" and can see it – whether intentional or not. Scenarios like this are of concern particularly where health or credit card information is concerned.

For risk inventory purposes, think about the situations in your business where someone is working with sensitive data and that data on their computer screen might be visible to others. These situations are easy to solve, but they should be consciously recorded as risks and dealt with. If your organization is ever audited from a security perspective, you'll appreciate having the documentation that you recognized this risk and dealt with it.

Inventory People

The term "People" refers to your employees, temps, contractors, volunteers, board members – everyone that has anything to do with your organization. If anyone has access to sensitive data, they are themselves a threat. They can be a threat because of using a poor password (which is controllable), they can be a threat by leaving data or information out where someone can easily take it. They can also be a threat by falling victim to a social engineering exploit – where one human being fools them into giving up their user-id and password so that an unauthorized person can gain access. The industry calls this phishing and it is a big problem.

List out every person with access to your computers, devices, applications and data – they are a risk.

Inventory System Access Control

Related to people is how you manage access to your computer systems, devices, applications and data. Many organizations take the easy approach and give full access for everyone to everything. This posture removes a number of potential barriers for efficient use of computers. Unfortunately, it also creates the most risk, partly because of the people aspect noted above.

For inventory purposes, make note of who has access to which computers, devices, applications and data. You may be surprised to find out that there are many people who have access to things that they shouldn't. Removing the temptation also removes risk of unauthorized access.

Inventory Other Technology infrastructure

The categories above cover many dimensions of potential risk in an enterprise. This element of Other Technology infrastructure is really intended to mean "everything else". This could be dial-in facilities, cloud or SaaS service providers (Office365, Amazon Web Services, Salesforce.com, etc.), live network connections to other organizations, firewalls, network load balancers, etc. Don't worry if you don't have these things – but if you do – put them on the inventory as a potential place of risk.

Assess the Inventory

With the inventory of the items above, assessment is simply going through each item in the inventory and asking the question "How can an unauthorized person get to the information on this item that we have to protect?"

At http://securityguide.blakeholman.com, under the Resources menu option, select Checklists. In the resulting web view, there is a document entitled "Risk Inventory.xlsx" which demonstrates sample information regarding an assessment of the inventory.

Step 2: Take Action – First Four Actions for Risk Reduction

No computing environment is perfect and completely without information security risk. The best that we can do is to employ good practices into our operation that keep the risk to a minimum given the human, time and financial resources at our disposal. That said, many organizations stick their head in the sand and hope and pray that they don't have an issue. As a good friend of mine once said, "Hope is not a strategy!"

Instead of hope, we can use our inventory and risk assessment as a guide to reduce our risk. If you haven't completed step 1 above (risk inventory and assessment), which is common for many organizations, I would implore you to take time to do it. It will inform many improvement opportunities in the future with clarity and focus. But even if you don't, the sections that follow articulate several simple actions that you can take to reduce risk, though they are not necessarily easy to accomplish. These actions are encouraged by the Australian Signal Directorate, a reference to which you can find at the end of this guide.

Application Whitelisting

Application whitelisting is the process of defining (and enforcing) that only certain applications are permitted to run on your organization's computers and devices. All other non-approved applications are prohibited. This is easy to say, not so easy to do, as it requires discipline to know what is running in the environment and staying up with updates, patches and such.

But – pulling it off makes a whole lot of security headaches go away.

Application Patching

Application patching is simply the process of making sure that all applications in the enterprise have updates from the manufacturer applied and distributed in a timely manner. While some version updates include updates to enhance capabilities, many updates these days are a race against the bad guys to fix security issues.

Some applications in particular are very, very risky to leave unpatched, as they are a reference point for many other applications or web sites. These extra risky applications include, but are not limited to:

- Adobe Flash
- Web Browsers (Internet Explorer, Chrome, Firefox, Mozilla, Safari, Opera, etc)
- Microsoft Office (Word, PowerPoint, Excel, Outlook, Publisher, OneNote and others)
- Java
- Adobe Acrobat and other PDF viewer tools

OS Patching

Like applications, Operating Systems in use have bugs and vulnerabilities all the time. When a vulnerability is discovered, there is a race between the bad guys and the manufacturer to get a fix (patch) out before anything bad happens. Of course, companies with poor patching / update processes are at much greater risk than those that implement patch updates as soon as they're available from the manufacturer.

Admittedly, applying OS patches and updates can be disruptive to users, particularly ones with laptops that want to shut their computers down and leave for the day. Murphy's Law says that the updates will happen when you least have the time to wait for them. Don't fall victim to the complaints from users and defer patches. Instead, develop a method to let people know what's happening so that they know what to expect and can navigate accordingly.

No matter what Operating Systems your computers run – patch them often. It's too risky not to do so.

Minimize Admin Privileges

Many organizations, as noted before, take the easy route and give their users full access to their computers. Some companies write bad software and require normal users to have full access privileges. Hackers and malware authors work to take advantage of these conditions.

Consider this: a user clicks on a web site with malware on it downloading the malware and attempting to run on your computer – if they don't have admin privileges, most malware will go nowhere. If they DO have admin privileges, it can begin to wreak havoc and create a bunch of cleanup work that could have been avoided.

To limit admin privileges, there are some simple steps that can be taken:

1. For each person that requires (and I mean truly requires) administrative authority on the system (Administrator or root, for example), set up a unique user-id for that person in parallel with a normal user-id account for them. Example: Bob has a normal user account name Bob11947, consider setting up Bob's admin account name as ADM_Bob11947.
2. When each person that requires an administrator user-id has been set up, change the password of the system level admin account so that no one can log into it.
3. Make sure that admin privileges are not granted via a security group. Domain_Users, for example, in a Windows environment, should not be a member of the Domain_Administrators security group.
4. Make sure that users are not granted local admin privileges on their user workstations, similar in concept to item (3).
5. Make sure that Service Accounts do not have Administrative privileges unless absolutely required, and then document that requirement as such.
6. For maintenance purposes, maintain a master list of the user-ids and service account ids that require admin privileges and verify each month (a security

maintenance activity) that only those ids are on that list. If a new user-id shows up on the list and the reviewer is not aware of it, it should be flagged as a potential security incident and reviewed.

Once Operating System admin privileges have been addressed, a similar procedure should be followed to review admin privileges in application systems. This is a concept called Role-Based Access Control and is aimed at ensuring that people only have access to the capabilities and information required for them to do their job and for which they are authorized. For example, if everyone with a login to an HR system has admin privileges (this is an absurd example to make the point), that would be bad. So – review the user access privileges and make sure that they don't have more access than they need.

Step 3A: Take Action – Establish Processes, Policies and Procedures

Policies

Policies define the expected information security posture of the organization and set expectations with users of the organization's systems about how they will behave when using the organization's systems or accessing the organization's data. The security control frameworks outlined at the beginning of this guide, as well as the security standards like PCI DSS, outline several areas where policies should be established.

Example areas (from the SANS Institute) for policy consideration include, but are not limited to, the following:

- Email policies
- Acceptable encryption technology policy
- Acceptable use policy
- Clean desk policy
- Data breach response policy
- Disaster recovery plan policy

- Digital signature acceptance policy
- Ethics policy
- Pandemic response planning policy
- Password construction guidelines
- Password protection policy
- Security response plan policy
- End user encryption key protection policy
- Bluetooth baseline requirements policy
- Remote access policy
- Remote access tools policy
- Router and Switch security policy
- Wireless communication policy
- Wireless communication standard
- Database credentials policy
- Technology equipment disposal policy
- Information logging standard
- Lab security policy
- Server security policy
- Software installation policy
- Workstation security for HIPAA policy
- Web application security policy

Each policy should outline its purpose, permitted use, prohibited use and consequences for failure to comply. Policies should be published, maintained and users of the organization's technology environment should be required to review the policies and acknowledge at least annually that they have read, understand and will comply with the policies of the organization.

Processes and Procedures

Like policies, processes and procedures set expectations for how the organization addresses certain elements of their information security program. PCI DSS and NIST 800-53, for example, outline several areas in which processes and procedures are expected, and which the organization should develop, if they aren't already in place.

Example areas for consideration include, but are not limited to, the following:

- OS patching processes and procedures
- Application patching processes and procedures
- Procedures and timing for updating the organization's risk inventory and assessment
- Procedures and timing for performing vulnerability testing, both internally and externally
- Procedures for engaging an independent third party for penetration testing purposes
- Procedures for conducting data backups
- Procedures for testing the data backups
- A Disaster Recovery plan and periodic testing procedures

As the organization increases its maturity, knowledge and experience with Information Security, new policies will be developed as will new processes and procedures.

A good Information Security program isn't a one-time affair – it is ongoing. It must be a consideration every single day in everything the organization does. In other words, security sensitivity must become a part of the culture of the organization.

The hardest part is getting the posture where the organization wants it. Up until this point, we've discussed things that can be done to address the reduction in risk (items in Steps 1 and 2 above). We have gone through 4 actions for risk reduction offered by the Australian Signal Directorate and we have a prioritized list of additional risk reduction opportunities from our risk assessment. We've also looked at putting policies, processes and procedures in place to support setting and managing expectations around what the organization does and does not do.

Next up – four items that can help shine more light on potential risks, which fall in the realm of "testing yourself".

Step 3B: Conduct Training For Everyone in the Organization

At this point, we've communicated to the organization what we're doing and why, we've assessed our risk, we've taking some key steps to reduce risk and we've come up with some new policies and procedures. Now is a good time to provide an update to the organization and make sure that everyone is informed and knows the actions they need to take in supporting the effort.

Make sure that everyone in the organization knows that patching is going to happen and sometimes it won't be convenient for them as an end user. The productivity hit of cleaning up from a breach is much greater than the possible inconvenience of waiting on patches to install on a computer system.

Make sure that everyone knows that their privileges are being limited on the system. It isn't because they are not trusted, it is because there is software running on their computers under their userid that isn't trusted.

And make sure that everyone knows of any new policies and procedures with which they have to comply and why. For example, the organization may begin requiring complex passwords of at least 8 characters, and they have to have at least one number, one capital letter, and one special character in them. If simple passwords were previously the norm, this can be a significant change for people and one which will likely generate a tremendous amount of consternation. If everyone is informed and knows clearly what they need to do to help with the initiative, there is a greater chance of success.

IMPORTANT NOTE: Ideally, communication and training about changes that affect computer users happens BEFORE the changes are implemented. It can be very painful to implement a change that is a surprise to end users, particularly if it is perceived as making their work harder to do. This will often generate backlash and the need to do cleanup / damage control, and is altogether counter-productive. Do what you can to prevent these situations by communicating well, communicating clearly and also making sure that there is Executive support for the program. Having strong Executive support for the program helps send a clear message to the organization that everyone is going to be involved in the program and the solution, even the Executive team.

Step 4A: Take Action – Test Your Environment

Think of the phrase "Trust, but verify". People are very trusting human beings, until other human beings give them a reason not to trust any more. This couldn't be more applicable than in the world of Information Security.

In the sections that follow, I outline four ways that you can test your technology environment and identify problem areas for resolution and further reduction of risk.

Backups - Try a Test Restore

When you have a security issue, the best thing you can have for recovery purposes is a good backup. Of course, you have to actually be taking backups in your environment in order to be able to restore data, so if you are not even backing up your systems, or you're doing business with people that aren't verifiably backing up your data – fix that first!

Assuming that backups are being conducted – make sure of a few things:

1. Make sure that they are backing up the data that should be backed up
2. Make sure that the backups are being taken at the right intervals for recovery purposes
3. Make sure that the backup data is secured so that it, too, is not a risk point

At this point, you should have a good degree of comfort with your backups, except for the "but verify" part of the phrase I used above. Every organization I have worked for has, at one time or another, had a situation where a backup was needed and it wasn't available.

Pick a file, a mailbox, a database, whatever you like and request that it be restored. For added comfort, consider doing a test restore of something from each backup environment in use: database, e-mail, files and such. For example, if you employ cloud services, have something restored from each provider to make sure that their stuff works!

When the restores are complete – review the result and make sure it is what you expected. Common problems at this stage include, but are not limited to, the following:

1. Backups are corrupt and your stuff can't be restored
2. Backups aren't conducted at the right interval and you can only get something "close" to the point in time you need
3. Backups don't go back far enough to get what you need (in which case you need to either change the retention period, or reset expectations on how long data is available)

And if you really want to be bold, restore an entire system from the ground up, as if you had a fire in your office and your server was destroyed.

In these scenarios, you'll learn very quickly how good your backups are. Once testing is complete, make note of the deficiencies and add them to your risk inventory. They need to be prioritized and addressed along with every other risk that remains for the organization.

Vulnerability Testing – External and Internal

Vulnerability testing is the process of scanning your computers systems (both those that face internal users and those that face external users) to see if they are vulnerable to common exploits in the security landscape today. There are a number of tools that can perform these steps in an automated fashion, but which may require some expertise to set up.

Once set up, though, they can be run at scheduled intervals (I suggest weekly) and give you an early warning to a potential risk, particularly if the vulnerability scanner knows about it and your vendors haven't given you patches for it yet.

As of the writing of this guide, http://www.1stoppciscan.com is an example of a provider that offers a service for running automated vulnerability scans against the external hosts of your environment. It provides a report of all the vulnerabilities found. This can be very useful for verifying configuration of web servers, firewalls, email servers and such, as well as patching levels. Vulnerabilities are present mostly because of a failure to patch or a failure to configure a system properly.

For internal vulnerability testing, non-profit organizations can qualify to use the industry leading product called Nessus. Like the external scanner, it can be set up to scan workstations and servers internal to an organization and offer guidance on patching and configuration issues. More information about

Nessus can be found at
https://www.tenable.com/products/nessus-home. Nessus is a
tool that required good technical expertise to set up and run. If
this is of interest to your organization, make sure that your IT
team or your IT service provider has the skills to utilize such a
tool.

Of course, not all issues are created equal. The output from
these vulnerability scanning exercises should be incorporated
into the overall risk inventory and prioritized along with
everything else. This will help make sure that the efforts of the
organization to reduce risk are focused on the areas where the
most risk can be reduced per unit of effort.

Penetration Testing (by a Third Party)

Like vulnerability testing, penetration testing is an incredibly
valuable testing effort to undertake, and one which is required
at least annually by the PCI DSS. Such a test should be
commissioned from appropriate third party organizations, the
result of which will be an indication of how easy (or hopefully
hard) it is for an unauthorized party to gain access to the
organization's technology environment.

A penetration test is the "but verify" step associated with
patching and vulnerability testing. You can patch and you can
run a scanner to verify that a vulnerability is not present, but
there may still be a way that an unauthorized user can get in.
The penetration test is where someone is actually hired to
break in. From this testing exercise, the penetration tester will
produce a report outlining what they did, how they got in and
suggestions for actions that your organization can take to
prevent others from doing so.

Social Engineering Testing

The last testing recommendation is to conduct what is called a
Social Engineering test. Up to this point, you've patched, you

scanned for vulnerabilities and you've had a professional try to break into your environment, hopefully with no success.

Now, it's time to test your people.

Most Social Engineering tests consist of three basic parts: an e-mail test, a telephone test and an "in-person" test. In the e-mail test, e-mails are sent to users in an attempt to get them to click on a web link or otherwise do something to give the attacker the ability to get into the computing environment with the user's credentials.

The telephone test involves the attacker calling a user on the telephone and explaining a situation which requires them to go to a web site or otherwise give the attacker access to their system or the user's user-id and password.

Finally, the "in-person" test involves the attacker showing up at a company location and trying to get into the facility and on the network. If successful, the attacker can plug in a computer, and, if not prevented from doing so (see Table 1 reference to "port locking on the LAN" entry), can scan network traffic and possibly steal data or "listen" for user-ids and passwords.

If the user population isn't trained to detect these scenarios and possibilities, it is common to have alarming results of a test like this. Don't be surprised if 30% or more of the population fall victim to the e-mail test, 25% or more fall victim to the telephone test and don't be surprised if the "in-person" test has a 50% or more success rate of "getting in".

Regardless of what the results are, the best medicine for these types of threats is training and awareness. Ongoing testing can contribute to reinforcing the lessons learned. Good Information Security is the responsibility of every person in the organization and it's something that should be kept top of mind all the time for the good of the organization.

Step 4B: Train Your Organization Again

The Social Engineering exercise will most likely uncover several more areas of concern from a security perspective. It is essential to train the organization again on the handling of e-mail, telephone call and in-person "attackers". The training should consist of identifying the warning signs as well as procedures on what to do if the warning signs are spotted.

I would encourage organizations to focus very much on identification of the warning signs, as that is where the biggest risk is. As far as action to take, people should be instructed to notify a central authority (person responsible for security, Help Desk, Office Manager – whomever is most appropriate for the organization) and leave it to that authority to handle the matter. The key to risk mitigation in this area is Identify and Report.

Step 5: Set Up for Ongoing Maintenance

To this point, the reader has conducted a risk inventory and risk assessment. They've implemented disciplined patching, application whitelisting and they've minimized admin authorities. They've implemented basic policies, processes and procedures and they've conducted several tests that embody the spirit of "Trust, but verify".

By having done these things, there is a material amount of risk that has been reduced, but not completely eliminated. Recall the opening to one of the sections above that read "No computing environment is perfect and completely without information security risk." That is still true. However, lower risk is better. And it is in that spirit that we continue to work in this realm.

Remember that a good Information Security program is not a one-time event. It is an ongoing commitment to doing the right things. And the best way to fulfill that commitment is to continually review and evaluate potential risks, address (remediate) them and do it again. I sometimes refer to this process as "lather, rinse, repeat."

Establish a Calendar

Don't rely on your memory for what needs to be done when, establish a calendar. A simple schedule in MS Excel will do, which can then be transferred to appointments in your business calendar once it is set.

Example items to include in the calendar are:

- Reviews of what users have admin authorities
- Reviews of backup logs to make sure that the backup software thinks it is successful
- Test restores to verify that the backups were, in reality, successful (Write-only backups are not very useful)
- Reviews of patching activities in the environment (both OS and applications)
- Reviews of security logs indicative of any non-whitelisted applications trying to run
- A scheduled refresh of the risk inventory
- A scheduled re-assessment of risk based on the refreshed risk inventory
- Scheduled reviews and updates of policy documents, process documents and procedure documents
- A schedule of vulnerability testing efforts and the review of their output
- A schedule of penetration testing efforts and the review of their output
- A schedule for user review and acceptance of security policies
- A schedule for user security training efforts

At http://securityguide.blakeholman.com, under the Resources menu option, select Templates. In the resulting web view, there is a document entitled "Admin Calendar Sample.xlsx" which demonstrates how an Administrative Calendar might look.

Some organizations set up their calendar so that it is a big bundle of activity once per year. Then, by the time next year rolls around again, they've got to re-learn how to do everything. Instead, consider setting up the activities so that some of them are done staggered throughout the year.

For example, if there are 12 policies that must be reviewed annually, review one per month. This will smooth out the effort and it will also reinforce the notion that attention to security is an ongoing effort. Likewise, if a policy review would result in a change in another policy, there is a chance to address it right away rather than potentially waiting a year to do it.

In addition to reviewing and monitoring, make sure that annual training and reinforcement of policies happens. The reality is that employees and business partners come and go in an organization. Every time a new person comes on board, there is someone that doesn't have the same frame of reference that everyone else has. Train them as part of onboarding, and then conduct annual training to make sure that everyone stays on the same page. Of course, conducting such things annually is considered the minimum – feel free to train and remind more frequently if you would like better results.

Execute and Keep Score

Once a calendar is established, execute it as scheduled. And make note of what is done or not done. You will likely find that what was planned may not be realistic. That's OK as you will get a chance to make it better for the next cycle.

In addition to noting what is done or not done, keep track of other details that are important for improving the posture of the Information Security Program. These might include the success rate of backups, the success rate of test restores, the number of vulnerabilities found with each scanning effort and things like this.

Keeping track of such details will allow the program owner to continually refine the program to ensure that it is constantly aimed at reducing risk for the enterprise.

Review at End of Year and Revise

Remember, there is no perfect program, and auditors know it. So, don't try to keep score to make it look like the program is perfect. When measures are out of line, take corrective action and demonstrate that the action returns the organization's posture to its desired state. What's important is that the organization does what it says it does and that it has good documentation to indicate diligence and focus on improving Information Security.

At the end of the year, look at the calendar and be honest about the plan. Was it too aggressive? Just right? Not aggressive enough? Did the organization implement additional things to further reduce risk and address items in the risk assessment?

Now is the time to adjust the plan, identifying those activities that will best ensure that Information Security is continually kept in mind and that every user is doing their part to fight the battle against the bad guys.

The review may yield that some activities are performed too frequently. Some may not be performed frequently enough. Activities may need to be added to the schedule.

Update the roadmap of next year's projects to ensure that the organization is continuing to move the needle on improving security. The risk assessment, vulnerability testing, penetration testing and possible social engineering testing should serve as a guide in this regard.

As a colleague once said, "Don't let perfect get in the way of better." Look at this annual review and planning exercise as a way of living in the spirit of continuous improvement.

Final Thoughts

Establishing a good Information Security Program is not an easy thing to do. There is a lot of information available about all the possibilities, which confuse organizations and often "freeze" them in a state of inaction. Don't be that organization. Utilize this guide to help your organization get started. Your security program won't be perfect, but you'll be actively on your way to reducing risk.

As the reader embarks on this journey, there are several additional thoughts to consider. These are:

1. If your organization is required to be compliant with HIPAA, it's all well and good to use this guide, but consider hiring a security auditing firm to conduct a HIPAA readiness assessment. Having implemented the things in this guide, you'll be off to a good start, but such an assessment will help prioritize the items in the risk analysis toward achieving compliance more quickly.
2. Don't forget about vendors and business partners of your organization. If they have your data and there is a breach, you're responsible. So, make sure that the people and organizations that you do business with also follow good Information Security practices.
3. If your organization provides services, you may be asked to comply with security requirements, maybe even have a certification like PCI DSS. Be aware and be prepared.
4. Remember that the cost of a data breach is the culmination of the losses to breached parties, the costs of an organization notifying every person whose data was breached (and handling it accordingly) as well as any Public

Relations costs or lost business costs associated with a loss in consumer confidence for the organization. These costs and losses can materially affect the ability of the organization to deliver on its mission.

Get started today – you'll reduce risk and learn more about what to do in the future. Your organization's future may depend on it.

For more information

The sections that follow provide background on and links to information about various Information Security organizations and references. In addition to these, gratuitous use of Google Search can provide the reader with countless references to ways in which other organizations have solved similar problems.

ISACA

ISACA is the Information Systems Audit and Control Association. Their web site is https://www.isaca.org. ISACA educates security professionals and administers several of the most influential security certifications in the industry. In addition, they are also a wealth of information in the world of information security.

ISC²

ISC² is the International Information Systems Security Certification Consortium and their web site is https://www.isc2.org. ISC² educates security professionals and administers several of the most influential security certifications in the industry. In addition, they are also a wealth of information in the world of information security.

InfraGard

Infragard is a partnership between the FBI and members of the private sector. Their web site is https://www.infragard.org. The InfraGard program provides a vehicle for expediting the timely exchange of information and promoting mutual learning opportunities relevant to the protection of Critical Infrastructure.

SANS

SANS refers to the SANS Institute and is an acronym for SysAdmin, Audit, Network and Security. Their web site is https://www.sans.org. SANS educates security professionals and administers several of the most influential security certifications in the industry. In addition, they are also a wealth of information in the world of information security.

NIST

NIST is the National Institute of Standards. As mentioned in the beginning of this guide, they publish a number of special publications in the area of Information Security through a group called the CSRC – the Computer Security Research Center. NIST Special Publications from the CSRC can be found at https://csrc.nist.gov/publications/sp.

ISSA

ISSA is the Information Systems Security Association. Their web site is https://www.issa.org. The ISSA is a not-for-profit, international organization of information security professionals and practitioners. It provides educational forums, publications, and peer interaction opportunities that enhance the knowledge, skill, and professional growth of its members.

HIMSS

HIMSS is the Healthcare Information and Management Systems Society. Their web site is https://www.himss.org. HIMSS is a global, cause-based, not-for-profit organization focused on better health through information and technology. HIMSS leads efforts to optimize health engagements and care outcomes using information technology. A number of resources of HIMSS have to do specifically with HIPAA security and compliance.

CHIME

CHIME is the College of Healthcare Information Management Executives. Their web site is https://www.chimecentral.org. CHIME is the professional organization for Chief Information Officers and other senior healthcare IT leaders. CHIME enables its members and business partners to collaborate, exchange ideas, develop professionally and advocate the effective use of information management to improve the health and healthcare in the communities they serve. Like HIMSS, a number of CHIME resources focus on HIPAA security and compliance.

NIST HIPAA Toolkit
https://www.nist.gov/programs-projects/security-health-information-technology

NIST CyberSecurity Control Framework (MS Excel Format)
https://www.nist.gov/sites/default/files/documents/cyberframework/framework-for-improving-critical-infrastructure-cybersecurity-core.xlsx.

NIST Special Publications
https://csrc.nist.gov/publications/sp800

References

1. MedPro. (2017). 20 Catastrophic HIPAA Violation Cases to Chill Your Blood. https://www.medprodisposal.com/20-catastrophic-hipaa-violation-cases-to-open-your-eyes/.
2. Focus On PCI. (2018). PCI Non-compliance Consequences.

http://www.focusonpci.com/site/index.php/pci-101/pci-noncompliant-consequences.html.

3. HHS.gov. (2018). Health Information Privacy. https://www.hhs.gov/hipaa/index.html.

4. PCI Security Standards Council. (2018). Official PCI Security Standards Council Site. https://www.pcisecuritystandards.org/.

5. Wikipedia. (2018). Family Educational Rights and Privacy Act. https://en.wikipedia.org/wiki/Family_Educational_Rights_and_Privacy_Act.

6. Wikipedia. (2018). NIST Special Publication 800-53. https://en.wikipedia.org/wiki/NIST_Special_Publication_800-53.

7. Wikipedia. (2018). ISO/IEC 27001. https://en.wikipedia.org/wiki/ISO/IEC_27001.

8. Australian Signals Directorate. (2018). Strategies to Mitigate Cyber Security Incidents. https://www.asd.gov.au/infosec/mitigationstrategies.htm.

9. National Institute of Standards Computer Security Resource Center. (2018). NIST Special Publications. https://csrc.nist.gov/publications/sp800.